VOICES OF THE WIND,

AND

OTHER POEMS.

THE

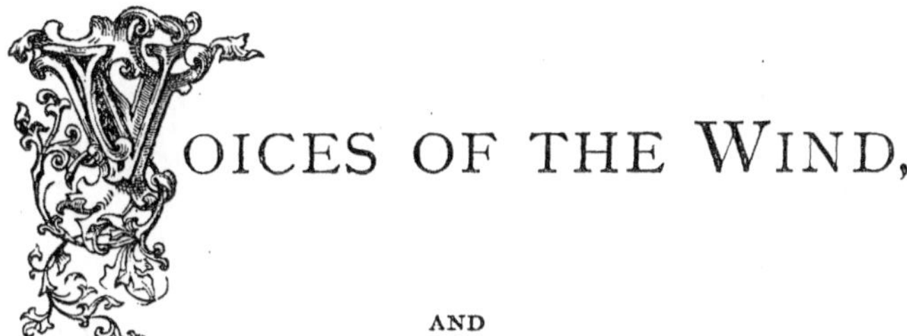

VOICES OF THE WIND,

AND

OTHER POEMS.

BY

P. FISHE REED.

CHICAGO:
E. B. MYERS AND CHANDLER,
87, WASHINGTON STREET.
1868.

CAMBRIDGE:
PRESS OF JOHN WILSON AND SON.

TO

FITZ HUGH LUDLOW,

BECAUSE HIS HEART IS BRIMMING WITH THE LOVE OF
ALL THINGS LOVABLE, AND WITH CHARITY
FOR ALL THAT ARE NOT,

This Tribute

IS OFFERED BY

THE AUTHOR.

CONTENTS.

MISCELLANEOUS.

SONGS.

VOICES OF THE WIND.

VOICES OF THE WIND.

FROM out the Boreal circle, from the valley of the
dew,
From the clouds of sapphire glory in the empy-
rean blue,
Cometh the gentle zephyr-wind upswelling from the plain,
Low humming, with its odorous breath, the summer's
sweet refrain.
It is coming with a lightsome step among the smiling
flowers,
Softly weaving song and beauty into all the glowing hours;
It dallies with the daisy, as it feeds upon the light,

And pets the peerless pansy through the silence of the night;
It creeps upon the water-cress that nods beneath the hill,
And trails its yellow tresses in the ripples of the rill;
It sleeps upon the pensive plain, where broods the turtle-dove, —
Where the rose and lily listen to the wild-bee's hum of love;
It wanders over all the land, and dimples all the sea,
And tips the lip of the loving one, and brings the kiss to me.
O wooing Wind, O winsome Wind, blow softly o'er the sea,
And hasten the ship of the loving one that's coming home to me!

In waving undulations, now, it skims the waters o'er,
And broods upon the diamond sand that sparkles on the shore;

Its breathes its fervent melody through all the living air,
And fans the cheek of beauty that is present everywhere;
It fans alike the high and low, the peasant and the peer,
And hums the hymn of Liberty to every listening ear;
And all the living things of earth reach up their lips of love,
To kiss the wooing zephyr-wind that gently floats above;
And love and life are mated, under all the azure sky,
As they listen to the music of the zephyr's lullaby, —
To the wily, wooing, winsome Wind that wanders every way,
So softly sighing with the soul through all the summer day;
The gentle Wind, that wafts the stately ship upon the main,
That is freighted with the loving one that's coming home
again.
O wily Wind, O winsome Wind, blow kindly o'er the sea,
And waft the ship of the loving one that's coming home to
me!

Oh, listen to the Borean breeze that sweeps across the
plain!

It is drinking up the zephyrs as the ocean drinks the rain;
It is coming with a fuller tone, that swells upon the air,
Like a million mingled voices that are whispering of despair;
And the troubled clouds are gathering, at the tempest-king's command,
While strange and fearful shadows weirdly skim across the land;
It revels in the lily-beds, where erst the zephyr slept,
And scatters into silver spray the dews the night hath wept;
And to and fro the roses sway, and, through the solemn dell,
It rudely rocks, in wanton way, the tiny lily-bell;
It hails the bending forest, and the creaking trees reply,
While the pallid leaves are whispering their terrors to the sky;
It swells the yielding canvas that so proudly spans the main,
And gloats upon the loving one that's coming home again.
O weary Wind, O dreary Wind, blow lightly o'er the sea,
And peril not the loving one that's coming home to me!

Oh, listen to the wailing Wind, that fills the panting air
With furious diapason tones that tell of wild despair!
It is coming, with a sturdy step, across the pallid plain;
It is breaking, into troubled waves, the broad and swelling
main;
It is bearing on its bosom that ominous refrain
Of the rumbling, roaring harbinger that goes before the
rain.
The traveller looks askant the sky, and reads the tale of
woe;
The startled herds upon the hills rush wildly to and fro;
The stately storm is marching on with force and fury rife;
The elements are marshalling their cohorts for the strife,
And the lashing, leaping lightning comes flashing through
the gloom,
While the closing of the darkness has the terror of the tomb.
O furious Wind, leave ye the sea, and rend the trembling
shore,
And give to me the kiss of death, but touch *his* lip no more!

O wanton Wind, O wailing Wind, save ye the swelling sea,
And spare, oh spare, the loving one that's coming home to me!

Oh! listen to the whirling Wind, that comes with battle-cry,
And scatters all the temples that are tottering in the sky;
The Borean bells are pealing over forest, hill, and dell,
And all the clamorous elements with furious anger swell;
The yielding waves are yawning over all the surging sea.
O God, protect the loving one that's coming home to me!
High and higher swells the tumult, and the frantic heavens choke
With the whirling and the swirling of the tempest-riven oak.
Oh, the clamor and the clangor of the quivering, shivering gale,
That is roaring, rushing, crushing, screaming, over hill and dale!

Oh, the thunder's rueful rattle! oh, the clang and crash and roar
Of the breakers, as they break and die, and feed the hungry shore!
There's a shivered ship a-sinking, there's a hissing of the spray,
While, down below, the yawning deep is yearning for its prey!
O rushing Wind, O crushing Wind, break not the shivering sea!
I cannot lose the loving one that's coming home to me.

Hark, what a shriek of sorrow! It is out upon the wave.
'Tis the fearful voice of agony uprising from the grave!
It is the prayer of the loving one who beats the foam in vain!
O God, protect! O wave, beware! O cruel storm, abstain!
Bring not upon my sorrowing soul a dark and nameless pain;

Bring not on thee, O murderous Wind, the cruel curse of
Cain;
Wreck nature into chaos, but for this bosom keep
That one, of all the living dead, out-tossing on the deep!
Oh, spare my love, and spare this heart, that's surging like
the rain!
And will that bosom never, never throb with mine again?
And must the star of hope go out, that erst was over-kind,
When we so fondly breathed our plight upon the zephyr-
wind?
The watching waves, with hungry strife, dart up their
tongues of doom,
While Death is grimly peering from the lightning-lighted
gloom!
O rushing Wind, O crushing Wind, break up the crumbling
sea!
For God has saved the loving one that comes no more to
me.

OKKIS-TUN:

AN INDIAN LEGEND.

OKKIS-TUN.*

ON Huron's mystic banks, in sombre shade,
When winter's twilight glanced upon the snow,
Three jovial hunters had their watchfire made,
And, gathering round its warm and ruddy glow,
Enjoyed that comfort hunters only know:
With jest and song, and with the good canteen
Which then was pleasure's boon and honor's show,
They wove their glee, the social hours between,
Nor recked if underneath the storm or starry sheen.

* Fire-spirit.

There is a glory in the hardihood
Of those old frontier-hunters who could tread,
With fearless step, the forest's solitude,
Despite its dangers, and with free-will wed
Its gloom for worse or better. The nuptial bed
New softness got with longer use, and dear
The dell where bear and bounding buck had fled;
And some fond memories linger round the rear
Of the last century, and its most bloody sphere.

The hunters pile the wood until the blaze
Is flashing in the restless eyes that prowl,
In sentry circles, in the purple haze,
Whence comes the sneaking wolf's discordant howl,
And the more bashful panther's modest growl;
While answers, from the height of some huge tree,
The hollow hootings of the moody owl.
They chime a tuneless chorus to the glee
Of the undaunted hunters in their revelry.

The senior of the party was quite hoary;
His limping limbs, and scarred head, front and rear,
(For he had seen somewhat of frontier glory,)
Bore the sad relics of a former year, —
The pay and pension of the pioneer;
And while the camp-fire lights the forest gloom,
And while the hunters sip the forest cheer,
They press the worthy veteran to resume
The bloody chronicles of Huron's day and doom.

Answered the old man, while a careless sigh
Escaped his bosom: From Superior's shore
To where the Alleghanies climb the sky,
I've seen somewhat of savage life (before
Civilization, with her sacred lore,
Diffused refinement through the forest gloom),
And in barbarian orgies joined the roar
To save me from a quite unpleasant doom,
And for a more refined procession to the tomb.

'Twas said, that, many hundred moons ago,—
Exactly when, tradition does not name,
But ere the Indian faced the pale-faced foe,—
The great Tun-Okkis, with a breath of flame,
Destroyed alike the Huron and his game.
Their valiant warriors and their boldest braves;
Their chiefs, who boast such prowess, strength, and fame,
Whose vanquished foes would fill a thousand graves,—
All flee before his wrath, while the whole nation raves.

Though wily arts and mighty arms they brought,
Besides some sacrifices to the moon,
Yet strength and stratagem availed them nought:
Soon as his thunder-voice was heard, so soon
Each victim sunk to earth, as in a swoon,—
A swoon of direful length—for to be brief,
Whene'er that voice was heard, at night or noon,
Whether the forest game or forest chief,
His heart's blood did outpour to dye the forest leaf.

Thus days passed on; the moons did wax and wane
And smile, although the sight was so absurd,
Of Huron's pest and his uncounted slain.
At last, in solemn conclave, council heard
The brave ones of the nation, who averred
Their willingness to quench this fatal Fire,
That had their nation's bravery so slurred:
It was their heart's most obstinate desire
To hurl him in the lake, but dreaded most his ire.

It has been told in story, sung in song,
Of the fierce courage of the savage race:
To poets only does the word belong;
For never beastlier coward, or more base,
Did hurl the dart of death with meaner grace
From skulking ambush, than these imps of hell.
True valor meets the danger face to face.
Courage! their traitorous souls did never swell
With flush of magnanimity, I know full well.

An aged hero, chief of Huron's nation,
With solemn voice then uttered his command:
Which heard, the braves leaped up in wild elation,
And scampered, screaming, over lake and land
With such outrageous roar that the firm hand
Of every foeman grasped his bow and blade
And burst away; new fire his fury fanned;
And ere the echo's answering voice was stayed,
Each summoned brave the old chief's mandate had obeyed.

I've heard that yell, joined in its chorus too;
For to their hate it was the antidote:
Yet my frail voice was but the kitten's mew,
When heard the din of the infernal notes
Of clamor bursting from their savage throats.
One night a cat, with wounds all furious grown,
With little ceremony and the votes
Of all, upon my naked back was thrown,
That I might better give the horrid war-whoop's tone.

In truth, I roared, — as well, indeed, I might —
Though many scars had made my back quite tough;
Yet, when I felt that woful scratch and bite,
I own that one such lesson was enough
To learn, at least, the war-whoop's gamut rough;
But long years after, when I did firmer plod
Along this lake and underneath its bluff,
Their heart's blood bubbled where the turf we trod, —
Oh, then I snuffed sweet vengeance from the steaming sod!

Revenge is sweet, and 'tis a sweet revenge
To gloat upon the prime aggressor's gore.
Be this denied, 'tis pleasant to unhinge
The spirit from the body of a score
Or two of his own ilk; nor keep in store
The pangs that prompt us to avenge a wrong;
For thorns within the heart will keep it sore,
And human passions, eke, are wondrous strong,
And will demand the rights which to our wills belong.

For those who draw from brute heart its life-blood,
Sate their own hearts with its familiarity,
Until at last, as sterner grows their mood,
The play of human blood is no great rarity.
In truth, we pioneers deemed it a charity,
Did we the red man's redder life outdrain:
To spill barbarian blood is no barbarity,
Since it would float him to a better plain,
And save his sturdy limbs from slavery's galling chain.

And he is not ignoble who would rather
Spill his life-blood in inglorious fight,
Than let it creep for tyrants, who would gather
Wealth and ease by others' toil. No blight
Of bondage blots his race. The right of might —
That self-same power that prompts each Indian soul
To be himself, and not another — will smite
The foe, and of his heart take ample toll
For right of way through realms his arms may not control.

I said the warriors met: and, at the spot,
There towered above them, like a statue vast,
The great Yandochis, chief of Wyandotte,
Whose furrowed brow was darkly overcast
With anxious care, and told the day was past
When he could wield the war-club; yet could sway
The entire nation with his guttural blast
Of eloquence, and teach them how to slay
The warrior and pappoose, and bear their scalps away.

"O braves and brothers! 'tis for you to know
The sacred warnings of the mystic trance,
When Areskoui* lifts the veil to show
The blazing beauty of his countenance.
Yandochis answered to the Burning Glance:
Claimed is unblemished chief, whose life is waning;
A thousand hearts his battle-axe and lance
Have hushed, who boasts a hundred battles' gaining,
And on his wigwam walls thrice threescore scalps remaining.

* The Great Spirit.

"And there must be a virgin of his name,
Whose spotless heart is pure as is the light
Of holy Heaven. The twain this Spirit Flame,
In the mid-hour of a moonless night,
Must quench in this dark water. From the height
That overhangs the lake's most northern shore,
His burning carcass must be hurled. If right
The deed be done, dwells Yandot,* as of yore,
Upon this soil; else drinks the thirsty sand our gore."

Yandochis moved not from his post-like posture,
But the keen glances of his eye round shot
Upon the tribe that he was wont to foster,
And, lo! each lip was curled, each heart was hot,
Each muscle strained with vengeance; yet was not
One warrior soul that dared the Okkis' ire,
Although they feared no earthly arm one jot;
And thus they spoke: "To quell this foe of Fire,
The nation hath no twain that answereth Heaven's desire."

* The ancient name of the Wyandotte.

"Behold thy chief!" Yandochis cried: "how vain
The hope of glory to his heart must be!
His wigwam shows the relics of the slain;
And his own daughter, bright Alankané,
The star-eyed maiden, child of purity,
At whose strange birth the twinkling stars down came,
To bless and fit her for her destiny, —
The Yandot princess falters not to aim
The daring death-blow at this shrieking Spirit Flame."

A brave then rushed the wondering warriors by,
And placed himself his mighty chief beside.
Vengeance was leaping from his restless eye,
And, with a voice of thunder, thus he cried:
"Alankané is pledged to be the bride
Of one who never plights his word in vain:
No Yandot warrior's claim must be denied.
Let her in peace in chieftain's care remain,
Till her Wenara hath this flaming Okkis slain."

The chief was silent; yet his stoic soul
Scarce brooked this insult to his faith, in gleams
Of light direct from Heaven. Such words made roll
His eyes in frantic glances; for his dreams
Were sacred to his soul as are the beams
Of daylight to the daisy. Dark suspicion
Leaps out from every look, volcanic streams
Upheave his quaking heart, at the derision;
Then wildly burst the words, and this is his decision: —

"Yandochis' child, whose heart his blood doth fill,
Embodiment of Heaven's love, — shall she
E'er fail to do great Areskoui's will?
'Tis his command: Alankané's must be
The maiden arm that sets our nation free.
Bring forth the sacrifice: let Yandots show,
In gory battle or in worship's glee,
That they their duty do, as well as know,
And never recreant prove when forward rush the foe."

Yandochis' word was law; and, peace restored,
A dog was placed the veteran chief beside,
Who gloated on the offering all adored.
With string of bark his mouth was firmly tied,
Then passed through flame until his reeking hide,
From drooping tail to fiercely snarling snout,
Was hairless as an eel. Thus deified,
Was placed upon a pole, while warriors shout,
And chant their sonorous song, his blackened form about.

SONG OF THE SACRIFICE.

I.

DEATH to Tun-Okkis,
The thunder-tongued foe,
Who bringeth Yandochis
The flame of his woe!
And now shall arise
The smoke and the savor,
And we shall find favor
In the sacrifice.
Dance to the doom!
The yellow sun leers at the gloom,

The hazy moon measures the blue,
And the stars are true.
Wa-ho-no-win! * Unk-ta-hee,†
Hear our song, and set us free.

II.

From the heights of the mountain,
From the lake and the wood,
By the tremulous fountain,
Where the wood-pigeons brood,
The wail of the warrior,
The moan of the maiden,
On the breath of Kee-way-din, ‡
Is laden with sorrow.
Dance to the doom!
The yellow sun leers at the gloom,
The hazy moon measures the blue,
And the stars are true.
Wa-ho-no-win! Unk-ta-hee,
Hear our song, and set us free.

III.

The bright eyes glisten,
That shall set us free,

* An exclamation of sorrow. † The god of battle.
‡ The north wind.

Like the stars, when they listen
To Alankané.
The smoke and the flame
The wild dog is breathing,
Up-curling, upwreathing,
Is Manitou's name.
Dance to the doom!
The yellow sun leers at the gloom,
The hazy moon measures the blue,
And the stars are true.
Wa-ho-no-win! Unk-ta-hee,
Hear our song, and set us free.

IV.

Fair one of Yandochis,
Thy spirit is strong,
And thine arm, from Tun-Okkis,
Will free us ere long.
Be snake-like thy tread,
And banish thy sorrow,
And the dawn of the morrow
May break on the dead.
Dance to the doom!
The yellow sun leers at the gloom,
The hazy moon measures the blue,
And the stars are true.

Wa-ho-no-win! Unk-ta-hee,
Hear our song, and set us free.

V.

In the deepest recesses
  Of the surging lake,
Where the tortoise caresses
  The slimy snake,
  Through the sprayey foam,
Hurl this foe of the forest.
When our need is the sorest,
  Avenge our home!
    Dance to the doom!
The yellow sun leers at the gloom,
The hazy moon measures the blue,
  And the stars are true.
Wa-ho-no-win! Unk-ta-hee,
Hear our song, and set us free.

VI.

Then death to Tun-Okkis,
  The thunder-tongued foe,
Who bringeth Yandochis
  The flame of his woe!

And now shall arise
The smoke and the savor,
And we shall find favor
In the sacrifice.
Dance to the doom!
The yellow sun leers at the gloom,
The hazy moon measures the blue,
And the stars are true.
Wa-ho-no-win! Unk-ta-hee,
Hear our song, and set us free.

O Superstition, thou round-eyed foster-mother
Of horrors all too horrid to be spoken!
Oh that some mighty power thy curse could smother,
As thou hast smothered souls, and basely broken
The bonds of human peace! I pray unwoken
May be thy sleep, if thou shouldst sleep; yet never
Has prophecy once dared to give a token
Of such blest time. No Archimedean lever
Can lift the deep, dead weight that bears us down for ever.

The wild and sacrificial song is o'er,
And frantic merriment begins to flow,
Where headstrong vengeance ruled the hour before;
The moaning dog is freely eaten now, —
An emblem of the mercy Yandots show.
Such rites as these are not the right of way
To realms of modern Hurons' Manitou;
But when Algonquins held despotic sway,
In savage might, o'er tribes that since have passed away.

If Yandots' statutes *had* such horrid modes,
As by their vague tradition is related
In legends wild, they're banished from the codes
Of modern Hurons, who — though wisely hated,
For their blood-loving souls are never sated —
Are pinks of patterns to all brutal breeds
Who meet them life for life. So some have prated;
Yet, in good sooth, the fabled demon's deeds
Of horror well befit these fiends whom Fury feeds!

When moody midnight spread her dusky pinions,
In solemn silence over lake and fell,
The self-doomed martyrs, Heaven's holy minions,
Had reached, with stealthy step, the demon dell
Where slept this pest of Huron in his cell.
With wieldy war-club, Yandot's hoary sire,
With hot heart-throbs, which he disdained to quell,
Approached with awe the couch of sleeping Fire,
To wreak upon his head the injured nation's ire.

A maiden arm arrests the fearful blow;
For they must follow Heaven's just decree,
And *she* must deal the death to Yandot's foe.
For this bright star-child, fair Alankané,
Drew from the heart its life-blood, just as free
As love throbs from her lovers, when there shone
The Cupid daggers in her midnight e'e.
In one hot, gory gush, one guttural groan,
The modest might of that mild maiden arm was shown.

Let poets prate about the beauteous squaw,
Her magnanimity and proud pomposity,
Her soul-lit eyes and chiselled lips, and draw
Delightful pictures of this mad monstrosity;
Yet if a nose out-bulged with animosity,
And eye that gloats on torture, blood, and death,
And mouth whose breadth could munch your corporosity
With savage greed, be types of beauty, faith!
They're welcome on such brutal belles to waste their breath.

There is no beauty in a wicked thing;
There is no beauty in a selfish feature;
And all such hideous symbols can but bring
Disgust to every honest heart. No creature,
If born of brute or human, holds his nature
In borrowed forms; but like from like is true
Of soul and body, as it is of each or
All the things with which the zones may strew
The earth: the Indian's soul and skin's alike in hue.

No more the weird Tun-Okkis cursed the dell;
But the blue bosom of the lake did bound
With rapid throbs, when there upon it fell
The victim and the victors. All were drowned;
For of this trio, never one was found.
But some moons after, so tradition saith,
When Hurons dared to tread the tragic ground,
They buried sundry implements of death,
Like those by which some thousands since have lost their
breath.

WACHUSET:

A STORY.

WACHUSET.

PART FIRST.

EOLUS slumbers in his mystic cell;
The Borean breezes rest awhile from duty;
The venturous zephyrs wander from the dell,
To toy with Flora where she sits in beauty;
The landscape lies abloom. In fresh perfume
The glad hours woo and wonder all the day;
With busy fingers, in their mystic loom,
They weave the gorgeous garlands for the rosy-favored May.

Above the rivers, above the rills,
Above the slopes of the wooded hills
Whose green waves roll with a ceaseless sigh;
Where the bald cliffs cleave the tender sky,
And the gray-grown rocks like sentinels stand
Over the belts of the busy land,
While rigid and cold and stern, they view
Alike the storm and the summer blue,
I stood; and gazing down the vale,
Listened to the simple tale
That now I tell.

'Twas summer-time,
When all the days are full of rhyme,
When zephyrs fan the forest bowers, —
The choral halls of plumèd throats, —
When the humbird kisses the flushing flowers
With giddy delight, and the nectar sips
From their voluptuous, pouting lips;

When all the voices of the hours
  Are tuned to music notes;
And along those vales that slanting lie
Under the sheen of the summer sky,
Embroidered with beauty everywhere,
And drinking light from the amorous air,
The violet and the purple bell,
The clover blooms and daisies rare,
  Internestling in the light,
Pant, as their odorous bosoms swell
With silent delight, like those who tell
  Their loves in the silent night.

And these are the days of love and bloom,
The halcyon time of flushing youth,
Who never dream of the winter's gloom,—
Who never dream, kind Heaven's ruth,
Of the visionless sorrows, that one by one
Canker the heart as life goes on;

But blithesome through the summer way,
Will youth and pleasure meet and play;
And the spirits of light and gentle love,
Whose home is the palpitating air, —
The invisible world about and above, —
Watchfully ward from the youthful heart
The evil wicked ones impart;
But the kelpies who love the lonesome ways,
And gloat on sorrow's gathering haze,
Hide from the flowery summer's bloom,
And revel in the mountain gloom.

A noble youth lived in the vale
  Under the frowning mountain,
And his soul was as grand as the towering cliff,
  And as pure as its crystal fountain;
And a maiden there was who loved this youth,
  And the youth he loved the maiden,
And they flushed and thrilled, yet never knew,
As on the busy moments flew,

That each with the other's love was laden;
And the voice of their lives went to and fro,
Whispering melodies soft and low,
But never a syllable more than this,
Uttered the lovers of this sweet bliss.

They climbed among the clefted rocks
  Where the honeysuckles climb,
And tenderly crowned each other's brows
  With the wreaths of summer-time;
They plucked wild flowers from the sylvan bowers,
And sheltered themselves from the thunder-showers
  In the caves of the mountain-side,
And dreamed the fabulous legends o'er
Of the barbarous savage's mythical lore
  When the warrior was in his pride.

The laughing water-brook that leaps,
    In gleeful pranks,

Adown the mountain's broken steeps
    And mossy banks,
They chased along the cedar maze,
  Listening to its tinkling lays,
While their hearts' syllables kept time
To its tintinnabulary rhyme;
For like the brook the heart will dream
Till lost in life's maturer stream.
Over the meadows, along the rills,
Or under the rifts of the rocky hills,
Or on the lagoons where the lilies lay,
Wherever his footsteps led the way,
She followed him, with never a thought
But of the pleasure the present brought:
Their life was a day with no cloud above,
Each day a life of the purest love.

Thus hand in hand they walked together
Through all the bloom of the summer weather;

And as the odor fills the sense,
Love filled their hearts with his influence;
And they followed their lives with a brook-like dream,
  Through many a winding way,
As joyous as the mountain bird
    The livelong day;
Nor ever there came an evil sprite,
Nor malignant being that haunts the night,
  To whisper a wicked thing;
For their souls were as pure as the ether light
  In all their wandering.

And a joyous band of spirits bright,
  Linked hand in hand together,
Followed the lovers here and there,
Followed them faithfully everywhere,
  Through fair and stormy weather;
Like guardian spirits, they watch and pray
Over their innocence night and day;

While the light-winged zephyrs, with anxious care,
Tenderly sprinkle the happy pair
With incense. Oh! the days were fair;
For the odorous brow of the summer queen
Was pranked with beauty, and everywhere
Her jewelled blooms and garb of green
  Swelled up in the violet air;
And from early morn till dewy eve,
  To the beat of their bosom's rhyme,
This web of love the lovers weave
  With never a thought of time.

He was to her as the golden day
  To the flushing flowers,
Filling her life with a summer way
  Through all the glowing hours, —
Filling her soul with the thrill of life,
  As grandeur fills the throne;
He was to her another world,
  Its glory all her own:

And she to him as the rippling sea
  To the starry sky above,
Holding his tremulous beauty there
  In the depths of her placid love;
For as the heavens their glory bloom
  Within the crystal tide,
So he in her: he was her heaven,
  And she his mirrored bride.

So they sang together the song of life, —
  The youth and this matchless maiden;
And they murmured the music of innocent love,
Till the very air about and above
  With the odor of love was laden.

Oh! is there above this transient night,
  At the going-down of time,
A dawn of life for longing souls
  In another youthful clime,
Where youth and innocence dwell, as here,
In the summer of Love, where the skies are clear?

PART SECOND.

THE Borean bell has tolled the lowly vespers
Of the pent-up winds, who pensive grieve
In mournful sweetness, while their smothered whispers
Are so softly breathed to summer eve;
For whirlwinds, big with power, await the hour
When they shall burst their mountain bands asunder,
And ravish Beauty in her blooming bower,
And howl her dirge o'er hill and dale in tones of mighty
thunder.

The red-lipped summer has ceased to smile,
The birds have forgotten their song,
The skeleton forest is bloomless, while
The north wind cometh along

Hoary and chill, o'er hill and copse,
Like the demon that blights our youthful hopes, —
Hopes that bloom in life's summer-time,
And wither beneath the winter's rime.
'Tis night, and the night is dark and chill;
There's a helmet of sleet on the sombre hill;
There is storm above, there's foam below,
And the air is oblique with cutting snow;
The clarion winds, in clamorous notes,
Are answered back from the tongueless throats
Which gape from the cavernous precipice
That pouts its lips for the stormy kiss.
'Tis the noon of night, and the creaking trees
Are knelling the hour to the boisterous breeze;
And the moody owl, with solemn eyes,
Has sheltered himself from the turbulent skies,
In the dusky holes of the cedar-tree,
And responds *tu-whoo!* to the jubilee.
Each answers the other with right good will

From the clamorous air and the groaning hill;
Each answers the other with all his might,
Shrieking and creaking the noon of night!

And there is a darksome demon clan,
Who gloat on the storm and shivering snow,
Whose only joy is the hate of man,
  Whose bliss is to work him woe.
Their eyes are black, and their hearts are chill
As the clouds that brood the dewy hill;
And they are glib, and they are glad,
  And have been many a day;
For a blue-eyed maiden has been sad,
And the kelpies ken her raving mad,
  As she wanders the woodland way.
And they giggle and grin in mad delight,
And they harass her soul with all their might,
And they chime and chant to the storm-king's rant,
  In a horrible roundelay.

KELPIES' CHORUS.

I.

  HARK! hark! the night is dark,
  And the night is chilly and drear;
Mortals may dream by the fire's red gleam,
  But never may venture here;
Yet we are the demons who proudly dare
To brook the breath of the stormy air!

II.

'Tis a gala-night on the mountain's height,
Old Boreas bellows with right good-will:
Oh! never before has the choral roar
Of the stormy minstrels been so shrill!
How the pines careen, with their plumes of green,
As they bow to the storm with a haughty mien!
How their long trunks creak a staccatoed shriek,
To the chorus that comes o'er the mountain-peak!
And the tenor that rolls through their whistling limbs
Is the wail of the woodland's chordless hymns.

III.

The earth is soaked, and the pathways choked,
And the fountains are seething, but not with heat;
Caves echo the tones of the forest groans,
And the tremulous boughs are bathed in sleet.
How the frozen rain, with might and main,
Is beating the boughs where the birds have lain!
The gloom is our cheer; and, if mortal is here,
We will harass his soul with a horrible fear.
And the visions that pass through his wildering brain
Are dark as the phantoms of Death's domain.

IV.

Hark! hark! the night is dark,
And the horrible hour is full of cheer;
Mortals may dream by the red fire's gleam,
But never may venture here;
Yet we are the demons who deftly dare
To buffet the breath of the stormy air.

The echoes of the kelpies' song
Had reached a gentle faëry throng;
And quick as lightning cleaves the sky,
Or thought from place to place may fly,

That faëry group stood hand in hand,
Amid that darksome, demon band.
And as the wrong avoid the right,
Or gloomy shadows flee the light,
The demons hide in the humid hill,
And listen to the spirit trill;
For nymphs and fays, with voices rare,
  Joined in the melodie,
While echoed through the stormy air
The measures of their minstrelsy.

The demon shadows deeper shrink
Beneath the precipice's brink,
Till the noxious air of the dank ravine
Hideth all but their ghastly grin;
While the faëry group in silvery vapors
  Down the mountain sways,
Until their graceful outline tapers
  To minuter rays.

They are hieing away through the weeping wood,
They are going down on a mission of good ;
For a sad one is wandering through the gloom :
  Zenilla is treading her wonted way,
For she has been under the kelpies' doom
  For many a darksome day ;
And there is a stranger down in the glade,
Lost in the depths of the cedar shade.

A serpent path the rugged hill
  Encircles around and about,
And the weary traveler, cold and chill,
Has followed the way with right good will
  Since the daylight hath gone out.
But wrong goes he, with eager rush :
The path leads not to a downy rest,
But through the fern and berry-brush,
And tangled brier and twisted vine,
Stubbornly, sternly crossing his line,
  Winds up to the mountain's crest.

He is coming home from a foreign land,
He is coming to claim the plighted hand
And the heart that was pledged when life was new,
If she, perchance, the affianced bride,
Remembereth the love that time hath tried,
The love that to her has proved so true.

Dull in the darkness there was a glimmer, —
The fox-fire's phosphorescent shimmer;
Wherever he trod, the lambent flame,
On soil or sod, it went and came,
    Flickering, flashing,
    Leaping and lashing
The mossy stone and the wood decayed;
And it weirdly, wildly danced and played,
  Where his footsteps fell,
Like a will o' the wisp in the solemn dell,
Flickering, flashing all the way;
But there was no heat in the cheerless ray.

Ill he rests his aching head,
  Pillowed upon a stone;
Chill he lies, for his cavern bed
Is dark as the land of the silent dead, —
Dark as the tomb where dead men lay
In the mouldering coffin dank and gray, —
    Alone, alone,
Under the gray and the dripping stone,
While the moments fall from the waves of time,
As falls the mist of the winter's rime.

But the fitful dreams that o'er him steal
In strange confusion, but dimly reveal
The spirit war that rages between
The cruel kelpie and fairy queen;
For fairy voices in music streams,
That never are heard except in dreams,
Feebly, faintly rose and fell
So softly, the dreamer could scarcely tell

If it was the breath of a loved one's sigh,
Or the hum of a mother's lullaby.

Is it a vision that fills his brain,
  That makes his heart to beat?
Or is he living o'er again
  Those days so passing sweet?
He may not tell, it is so real,
If it is a dream of the soul's ideal,
For there are times 'twixt waking and sleeping,
When the laggard will is sentry keeping,
When the spirits of light, who inhabit the air
In the mountains and valleys and everywhere,
May enter the mind with their subtle breath,
And paint the mystery of life and death;
While the warp and the woof of the present and past
  Thrill the sense with images vast.

What though his aching limbs are chilled?
His swelling bosom is tuneful filled

With memory's music streams;
Now like a waterfall the flow,
Now like the eddy's whirl below,
That in the sunlight gleams,
They whisper when his heart was light,
And when his life was new,
Another fond heart day and night
Beat with his so true,
That did they throb apart or near,
Did they beat in woe or weal,
But one throbbing could they hear,
But one palpitation feel.
Yet a maiden's love may wax and wane:
Ah! is his cherished love in vain?

There's a sound of music — a plaintive wail —
Borne on the breath of the reckless gale;
'Tis like the music of many rills,
And its echo all the cavern thrills,

And its richness fills the traveler's ear,
And he springs from his couch, but not with fear.
Sinking, swelling, rising, falling
  In its cadence sweet and low,
Like the hum of loving voices
  He had heard so long ago, —
  Sinking, swelling, soft and low,
  Like the voice of long ago, —
It tells a tale with sorrow laden,
Tells of the grief of a love-lorn maiden,
Tells how the heart of a beautiful one
By love was made, by love undone.

Zenilla's is that voice of woe:
The kelpies have tuned it to the flow
Of their pitiless shriek. They have lured her away
From love and bloom to the mountain gloom,
  Where the desolate shadows stay;
And to and fro, through her living tomb,

She wanders, heedless of all but the song
Herself may sing of her bosom's wrong,
  When the light of her life went out;
Like some sweet bird torn from its mate,
And fluttering in its prison grate,
  Knoweth no joy without.

In wild refrain that thrilling strain
  Is borne with frenzied fleetness;
'Tis hushed, and now returns again,
  Smothered into sweetness;
And the song to the traveler's eager ear
Has shaped itself distinct and clear,
And his heart beats fast with the fresh blood's heat,
And his pulses quicken at every beat;
Awake and alert his sense may be,
But he may not fathom the mystery.

  A light in fitful flashes
  Streams into the cavern room,

And now the flame of a flambeau lashes
  The quick-retreating gloom,
Till the hurrying shadows fly with affright,
Like guilty spirits that hate the light,
  To the deepest nooks of the cave;
While glancing from each dripping stone,
Fantastic forms of fire-light shone,
  Like the moon on a rippling wave,
And they lapped up the darkness, here and there,
Till the dewy-walled cavern was all aglare.

A sweet pale face, an eye of blue
Shyly peering the cavern through,
A queenly figure, lithe and light,
Weirdly outlined against the night,
  Greeted the stranger's vision;
And he felt, as he gazed on the image fair,
Some spirit of love, still draped in the air
  That fans the blest Elysian,

From its ethereal world of bliss
Had sought the wildest part of this.

The maiden glanced the cave around,
And then, with measured move and slow,
As if in fear of lurking foe,
She placed the flambeau on the ground,
And, standing beside its ruddy blaze,
She fixed on him her searching gaze.
"Stranger, what spirit hath beguiled
Thy footsteps to this mountain wild?
Knowest thou not I am its queen,
And claim for my realm its groves of green?
Comest thou from a foreign land, —
The bearer of a court's command?
Then vain the mission. No fealty I
To other powers may own;
Return, and take them this reply:
I live and rule alone!

My kingdom is the solitude;
My castle walls the solemn wood;
  The ivied cliff, my throne."

The stranger marked the wild unrest
That rankled in the maiden's breast,
And kindly spoke: "Love's guiding star
Hath led me to these wilds afar,
  To seek my childhood's home;
To dwell again beneath its skies,
And from the light of lovelit eyes
    No more to roam."

"This dreary wild and mountain glade
But ill befit so fair a maid:
Come, breathe to me thy bosom's woe;
Whisper softly, and tell me low,
Of thy days of love, thy days of bloom,
Ere first thy footsteps sought this gloom,

And I will listen till the morrow's
  Breaking bid me go, —
With no thought of gentle slumbers, —
Listen to the mournful numbers
  Of the grief that fills thee so.
Tell me, maiden, of thy sorrows
  In the days of long ago."

"Love! it is a gentle word,
The sweetest, mortal ever heard,
  But it has come too late;
And yet it traces on my soul
  The picture of a fairer fate:
For the odor fills the blossom
  When its leaves are crushed and torn;
So the yearning of my bosom
    Is not gone.
I thank thee for that blessed word;
It wakes the echo of music heard

When life was in its May.
Thou seemest like a star to me,
That hath left the blue where the angels be
To light my lonely way
To thy beautiful home in the world above,
And lead me again to youthful love.

"What boots it to me, if they call me crazed,
Down in the world of fashion;
If they secretly hint that my soul is behazed
With a love-lorn fantasy's passion, —
With a fancied love of a heartless one,
Who hath my trusting heart undone?
For they whisper about
That the idol of my childhood's dream
Hath put the light of my reason out.

"I may not tell of that bliss divine
That thrilled this pliant heart of mine,

When in the days of long ago
It flushed with beauty from above,
And revelled in a world of love;
But of the word that worked this woe,
And drove me here, is thine to know."

PART THIRD.

EOLUS mounts his car, and Boreas fills
With furious, howling storms the earth and ocean,
And drives Collina from the trembling hills,
To gaze with wonder at the strange commotion;
For ocean, hill and plain must feel the bane
Of storm and tempest, as in wild elation
Their reckless arms do strive with might and main
To strew the fresh and blooming earth with ghastly desolation.

Like the whirlwind laden with sweet perfume,
Like a warrior maiden in virgin bloom,
Like the altar destroyed by its own incense,

Was this dual influence
On the wondering traveler's awakened sense;
With half of gladness, half regret,
Since first the vision he had met;
And the lonely night went moaning along,
While he listened to her song, —
Listened to the mournful numbers
Of her sorrows one by one,
With never a thought of gentle slumbers,
As the night went sighing on.

Oh! why should I attempt to hide
The sin of an angry father's pride,
When, disobedient to his word,
A loved-one was adored?
I would that I was spared the tale
That wrings my bosom so;

Alas! it will not now avail,
  And yet the words will flow.
I know not why this night should bring
Again those days of suffering;
Yet something prompts me to relate
The story of my love and hate.

It was the word of a hoary sire
That set my loving heart on fire, —
A cruel father's act, that wrung
The tendrils of my love divine,
That to its idol fondly clung;
That wound around that sacred shrine,
As round the oak the ivy-vine.
My darling, he said, was mean and low,
Without a name or wealth or show, —
A beggar, boor, unfit for me, —
And never could rise to my degree;
As if he knew that heart's deep quiver

As well as I who dwelt there ever!
As if a world of wealth were weighed
Against the heaven that love had made!
I heeded not the pitying hours
That tallied on my soul its doom;
I recked not of the pitiless powers
That penned me in a dungeoned room.
I felt not, saw not, neither heard,
For my heart-strings were strained to breaking;
And since he spoke that angry word,
My eyes scarce rest from constant waking.
I fled, I know not how or when,
To wild Wachuset's wildest glen,
And in its gloom, with solemn vow,
I gave to grief my heart of woe.

I stood upon the mountain's crest,
Above the world I once had blest,
And overlooked the lawn where lay,

In silvery sheen,
Adown the valley far away, —
As fair as when I was its queen, —
My father's cottage on the green.
I hurled my malediction dire
Upon my hoary, hated sire!
A parent curse! Why should I not?
By him upon himself 'twas brought:
He hurled my reason from its throne,
And with it went a daughter's love.
A will, to all but me unknown,
Was left, — a will that none could move.

Burned in my heart prophetic fire,
That took possession of my breath,
And prompted me to curse the sire
Who gave me life, who gave me death.
Scarce the malison was uttered,
Ere the distant thunder muttered

A rumbling answer to my will,
Then boomed along the trembling hill!
And the valley bėlow, that a moment ago
  Slept in the sunshine warm,
Now frightened lay, draped in the gray
  Of the shadow of the storm.
And the spectre clouds, in angry strife,
Like demons who haunt a broken life,
Rose and fell in the frantic sky,
To the clang of the tempest's fearful cry;
While down below, in a world of woe,
The forest by the river's marge,
Like an armèd host, swayed to and fro,
  Bracing for the charge.
Brighter the serpent lightning shone,
And louder swelled the thunder's tone,
Till flash on flash so sudden came,
The hill was wrapped in sheet of flame.

Then came a voice from the surging deep,
That drowned the thunders with its roar;
And every cave and craggy steep
Flung back the echoes they could not keep,
And opened their hungry mouths for more;
As my bosom opened to a father's bane,
Then madly hurled it back again.
It was the blast of the whirlwind's breath, —
  The whirlwind savage and sore,
That rides on the horrible steed of death,
  From the bergs of the borean shore.
And he ravished the hill with frightful roar,
And glutted the air with clamorous notes,
Till wild confusion did outpour
From the mountain's thousand throats!
And the giant trees affrighted rose,
  And in the whirlwind eddied,
And rocks were torn from the repose
Where they for ages had been bedded!

I gazed upon the whirlwind's might,
And smiled exulting at the sight,
  And unappallèd saw,
Uprising in the stormy foam,
And madly lashing the murky dome,
The furious fragments of that home
  That I should know no more!

But why should I again rehearse
The horrors of that frenzied curse,—
That day of anguish, day of doom?
For all my kith, and all my kin,
Bowed to the whirlwind's wrath, and in
  Its vortex found a tomb!
But I never could have borne the blame,
I never could have borne the sorrow,
I never could have brooked the shame,
But that I felt, upon the morrow,
My soul's fond idol would come to claim

The heart that for him had drunk such horror.
Still that morrow never came,
Still I nurse my bosom's flame.
And many a night since then I've passed,
When loudly wailed the tempest's blast
Upon the rock where then I stood,
Upon the spot from whence I viewed
    That direful scene,
Which ghastly desolation brought
Upon my happy childhood's cot,
That erst lay sunning on the green.

Oh! what is this that thrills me so,
  Like joy and sorrow blended?
And what is this that whispers low,
With the tender voice of long ago,
  My day of doom is ended?
Is it a vision thou hast wrought
That thrills me with the during thought

That thou art he? O God, the bliss,
The bursting bliss, that floods my soul, —
That brings such ecstasy as this!
O rapturous love! O sweet desire!
Returning Reason's radiant light,
That kindles my thraldom's gloomy pyre, —
That breaks upon my bosom's night,
And drowns my senses in delight!

CONCLUSION.

THE kelpies are silent within the earth,
In the watery caves that gave them birth,
And the fairies are singing their sweetest lays
All along the lonesome ways.
The snows are feeding the verdured plain,
And the spring is climbing the slopes again,
To scatter the winter from the hills
Where erst were frowning skies;
For the sunshine all the valley fills,
That once was full of sighs,
And it daintily dots the sombre shade,
Under the forest trees,
Leaping so cheerily over the glade,
Where the buttercups bend to the breeze,
Down in the grass in the diamond dew,

On the rippling rill on its silver spray,
Tinging all with a golden hue,
And scattering diamonds all the way, —
Over the earth and through the air,
Scattering diamonds everywhere.
And while the blast of the winter goes,
The balmy breath of the summer blows,
Odored with richness, filled with the tale
Of love that blooms in the sleeping vale;
While over the lawn and over the lea,
Where Beauty is dancing full of glee,
The noble youth and the matchless maiden
Revel again in true love's Aiden.

THE SONG OF LIFE:

INNOCENCE; PLEASURE; AMBITION; FRUITION.

THE SONG OF LIFE.

INNOCENCE.

HIGH above the music of the soul,
When life's fair morn upon the world is dawning,
There is a spirit-bell's prophetic toll:
"One life only!" is its mystic warning.
Oh! is there not a power can stay the hour,
Or give us other life in full reality?
A food for each desire is Nature's dower;
Then why not, for the yearning soul, responsive immortality?

By the cradle's side there stood
  A mother fondly smiling,
As her infant child she viewed
(In a loving mother's mood),
  Thus the hours beguiling;
For this new life filled her sense
With a holy influence.

Gazing, dreaming, dreams of fame
  Flash upon her feeling,
Lighting up the vestal flame;
But the bosom hath no name
  For this rich revealing
Of its bliss, — this new creation
Of her fond hope's culmination.

Oh! maternal love is deep
  As the flowing river;
Swelling tide, but never neap,

Swelling onward, it will keep
  Swelling on for ever.
Blighted hopes her path may strew;
Still a mother's love is true.

Now the mother's heart is rife
  With the rising bliss:
"Ere he sees another life,"
(If he conquer in the strife,)
  "He shall be great in this."
And the swelling that is dwelling
In her heart, this tale is telling.

Hope inspired, she ponders never
  On the mystic warning;
Yet that life is fleeting ever,
Like the mist upon the river,
  Like the dews of morning:
Still the infant's innocence
Is a mother's recompense.

Mother's love! oh, blessed spirit,
  Flowing like the river!
More than token of our merit,
Best of all that we inherit
  From the blessed Giver!
Love and mother! treasure-laden,
They can make this earth an Aiden.

Reckless Change! O dull Decay!
  Are ye never sated?
Day and night, and night and day,
Bow we to thy cruel sway,
  Through ages still undated:
Say, is there no peaceful haven
Where thy deeds are never graven?

Love is blooming in her heart,
  Flushing it with gladness;
Cherish well, with cunning art,

Well; but love and life must part,
  Changing all to sadness!
O Love! O Life! so fondly mated,
Are ye never consecrated?

By the cradle's side, in grief,
  Sits a mother weeping.
Grief! It is a sweet relief,
Mourning for a life so brief,
  Mourning for the sleeping.
Hath the bud a future bloom;
Hope dispels the bosom's gloom.

Still a mother's love is deep
  As the flowing river;
Swelling tide, but never neap,
Swelling onward, it will keep
  Swelling on for ever.
Though her sorrows come anew,
Still a mother's love is true.

Knelling to her soul, again,
  Comes the solemn story:
"One life only!" Just begun?
Heaven, oh, let the goal be won!
  Else where is thy glory?
Life unlived! Then Hope's blest light
Faintly gleams beyond the night.

PLEASURE.

HIGH above the music of the soul,
When life's bright morn is to its zenith swelling,
"One life only!" cometh like the toll
Of funeral bell, the dirge of Childhood knelling.
O Youth! and must there be no life for thee,
Of blessed peace, beyond the turbid river?
Is all this flush of innocence to be
A solemn blank upon the page of Destiny for ever?

Oh! the morn of life is bright
As the blooming flowers.
Beamy Day may laugh at Night;
Yet the sum of life will blight

Childhood's rosy hours.
O Love! O Life! so fondly mated,
Are ye never consecrated?

Youth may plant, but Time will frost
Every fading flower;
Youth may hope, but, tempest-tost
On the shoals, the bark is lost, —
Lost the fleeting bower
Of their bosom's earthly treasures, —
Bubble joys and phantom pleasures.

Sad the hour that Pleasure brings,
At her final meeting;
Sad the song Experience sings,
Sadder still regret, that wrings
Hearts with high hopes beating,
For the knell of each to-morrow
Tallies on the soul a sorrow.

Still the morn of life is bright
  As the blooming flowers;
Beamy Day may laugh at Night;
Yet the sum of life will blight
  Childhood's rosy hours.
O Love! O Life! so fondly mated,
Are ye never consecrated?

Still that fearful threnody
  Comes in solemn numbers:
"One life only!" Oh! for thee,
Blooming youth, and can there be
  No voice to break thy slumbers?—
To call thee to some higher station,
For thy life's continuation?

AMBITION.

HIGH above the music of the soul,
That thrills the noon of life with wild elation,
When fierce Ambition, eager for the goal,
Goads on its votaries to the wished-for station,
There comes a plaintive wail that makes us quail:
"One life only!" breaks upon our dreaming.
O human Power! O Fame! and will ye fail
To crown us with that fadeless crown that erst was brightly gleaming?

There are castles in the air,
Beckoning us to glory;
Blooming, bright and wondrous, where,
If our footsteps wander there,

We may write our story;
But many paths, through mazy ways,
Lead us from the castle's rays.

Where the warrior rushes are
Fields of battle, gory;
And the crown he gathers there
Is the guerdon of Despair,
Gemmed with Sorrow's story.
Life for life! He takes away
That he never can repay.

And the miser's hoarded gold
Clogs his weary hours;
'Tis for this his soul is sold:
Rust and ruin, cankering, mould
All his manly powers.
Till his sordid life is done,
Mammon is his Eidolon.

And the anxious poet, gloating
  On his soul's ideal,
Of the present makes no noting,—
Heedeth not the pleasures floating
  Down among the real.
May he never grasp the treasure
Which his spirit strives to measure?

Hope will lead us on and on,
  Through life's mimic gladness.
When the day of bloom is done,
When the fancied goal is won,
  Cometh the night of sadness.
Starless night beyond the tomb?
Heaven forfend the fearful doom!

Still, beneath Ambition's load,
  Fostering gathering sorrows,
We plod the joyless, fabulous road,
Heeding not the cruel goad,

Through all the rayless morrows.
Heaven, is not the soul's ideal
Found in thee a treasure real?

Still the votaries of glory
Tread the thorny way.
When life's winter finds them hoary,
If the trumpet tell their story,
It is ample pay;
But ne'er comes the full fruition
Of their sibylline ambition.

Still the temple fades away
From each fevered vision;
Every step our feet may stray,
Every turn and every way,
Leads us from Elysiun;
Yet with earnest, mad intent
Toil we, till our life is spent.

Still the castles in the air
  Beckon us to glory,
Blooming, bright and wondrous, where,
If our footsteps wander there,
  We may write our story.
Yet the many mazy ways
Lead us from the castle's rays.

Still that song is murmured on,
  Mocking our ambition:
"One life only!" It is gone,
And the fame, so dearly won,
  Lost in airy vision.
O Hope! O Life! so sadly mated,
Are ye never consecrated?

FRUITION.

HIGH above the music of the soul,
When our hearts are sad and heads are hoary,
That plaintive murmur cometh like the toll
Of funeral bell, — the knell of human glory:
"One life only!" Is that life completed?
All things must have an end that are begun;
Have we no spirit-life. Time hath not meted?
O Heaven! where is thy glory if that goal is never won?

From the cradle to the grave,
The path is paved with sorrow;
From the cradle to the grave,
Man will make himself a slave

To each coming morrow,
Striving for that phantom treasure
Which his soul may never measure.

For the fame Hope pointed to
Mocks our toil and trouble:
'Tis the mirage that we pursue,
And the temple is not true,
Now a broken bubble;
Tell us, Fame, where is thy bliss
In a changing world like this?

Where the crown for which we strove?
Where thy promised glory?
Where the life and precious love
Which our earnest bosoms wove
In thy flattering story?
O Love! O Life! so sadly mated,
Are ye never consecrated?

All the deeds that we have done
  The ebbing soul revulses.
Ere the game of life is won,
The leaden blood is creeping on
  Through our leaden pulses;
Stolid apathy is hushing
All the burdened bosom's gushing.

The time is o'er, the day is past,
  The heart has ceased its quiver;
That which blooms must fade at last;
On the Shore we stand, aghast,
  And launch upon the River!
Eternal river shall it be?
Sailing on a senseless sea?

High above the music of the soul,
That warms our youth and fires our manhood's bloom,
And high above the thrilling tones that roll

Prophetic warnings of that fearful doom
Of dull decay that knells us to the tomb,
There is another Voice whose accents fire
In holier ecstasy our life's desire.
It is the ritornel of God's decree,—
The glorious song of Immortality!
O blessed Hope, in every bosom planted!
O blessed Song, to every bosom chanted
By angel voices, through the shadowed way
That leads to fairer clime and brighter day,—
That fills us with this sense of joy supernal,
That first and last our life is One, Immortal and Eternal!

PICTURES IN THE SKY.

PICTURES IN THE SKY.

PART FIRST.

UNDER the dome of the summer blue
A fleecy cloud floated in azure dew,
Moving along, by the breezes fanned,
Like a sylph of light in fairy-land.

'Twas the radiant queen of a kingdom rare,
That coursed through the calm of the upper air,
Throned in a temple of diamond mist,
Which the wooing heaven-wind tenderly kissed ;
And above and about, with banners bright,
Lay the pavilions of liquid light.

Her garments were fringed with a golden blaze;
And the delicate-tinted purple rays,
That blended the folds of her snowy dress,
Softened the whole to loveliness;
And the dewy shadows, that went and came,
With the luminous air were all aflame.

Upon her brow was a radiant crown
Of every jewel that man has known;
And all the glory the sunset brings
To beautiful shapes, and all sweet things
That people the air of the azure deep,
Passed like a pageant of gentle sleep.

And out in the valleys of golden dew,
Margined with forests of every hue,
Lay the lakes and the lilied lagoons,
That swelled to the light like silvery moons,
While many a fair isle daintily gave
Its amber leaves to the purple wave;

And the shimmering rivers and sparkling rills
Leaped from the rocks of the ruby hills;
While the gorgeous landscape, all aglow
With the light that was its life and show,
Floated along in the azure skies,
Like a dream of the poet's paradise.

The sky was flecked with a fleecy throng,
Drinking life as they moved along,
Sporting around in luminous rings,
Dissolving again to shapeless things;
Then, bursting into the amber light,
They strewed the way with jewels bright.

They brought rare flowers from the æther bowers,
And sifted them down in haloed showers;
And they wove the ruby vines between
The templed altars of their queen;
And every obeisance they made, it won
A different robe from the setting sun.

And they scattered the daisies and lily-bells,
Plucked from the empyrean dells,
About and before the imperial throne,
Where the jeweled pavement with splendor shone;
And there was a fountain of sapphire spray,
Sprinkling its brilliancy all the way.

And there was one of princely mien,
Who guarded with care his royal queen;
And save a gleam of silvery hue
That traced his outline upon the blue,
The stately knight was dark and gray
As the heavy mist of a winter day.

Yet his bosom heaved with royal pride,
Like the eager swells of the coming tide,
As he twined the wreaths she was proud to wear
In the liquid folds of her golden hair;
But across her bosom's voluptuous swell
His ominous shadow darkly fell.

And the maiden queen, with never a thought
Of the beautiful things the sunset wrought
To people her realm, nor the fading day,
That with her glory must pass away,
Nestled herself on his sombre breast,
Like a bird that goes to its evening nest.

PART SECOND.

UNDER the dome of the summer blue,
Under the land of golden dew,
In the far-down horizon's line of gloom,
The king of the tempest mocked this bloom;
And a frowning host, with warlike mien,
Menaced the realm of the lightsome queen.

And that host came up on the rising gale,
Clad in the robes of steely mail;
Out of the gloom where the thunders groan,
Scaling the crags of the misty zone,
With banners and foaming steeds, they came,
And their lances were made of the lightning's flame.

And they rose and fell in the murky deep
To the boom of the thunder-guns, that keep

The echoing clouds repeating it where
They press through the palpitating air,
Surging and seething and swelling through
The foamy way to the dome of blue!

And there was a charger with flowing mane
And reeking sides, that led the train;
And his stately rider, the king of the gale,
With a burnished crest and a silver mail,
Proudly rose to the shimmering light,
Like the phantom form of a demon knight.

And that feathery cloud,—that midnight stain,—
Half-hid in the depths of the surging rain,
Now rolling with such a voluptuous swell
Into the light, and down the dell
Of dismal clouds, is the queen of that king
Who, conquering, rides on the tempest's wing.

The ravaging army came on, amain,
Till they reached the zenith,—a clamorous train,—

Drinking the dews of the fairy land,
Destroying all with the ruthless hand
Of a vandal horde, while, under all,
The delicate rain-drops gently fall.

They have compassed the queen and her retinue,
They have blotted her bloom from the dome of blue;
Her kingdom is dark with the coming doom,
Her land of dew is a land of gloom;
And a muffled murmur of wild despair
Runs through the ranks of the ravenous air.

And the stately knight who plighted her
When draped in golden gossamer,
When, all abloom, she shared her throne
And her maiden love with him, is flown.
Out in the surge of the shadowy way,
He is mocking the love of a fairer day.

The battle is past, and the freshening shower
Has sprinkled a diamond in every flower;
And that luminous circle that spans the sky,
Like a bow of promise to all that die,
Is to the queen a crown more true,
That never was seen when the skies were blue.

'Tis thus we are pressed in the battle of life,
'Tis thus we are compassed about with strife,
While love and glory, and all things fair,
Are swept away like a world of air;
And the fairest of all whose hearts are warm
Must bow to the blast of Death's wild storm.

And when the battle of life is o'er,
And the beautiful earth is ours no more,

May we not find, in some rainbowed bower,
A perishless diamond in every flower;
And a fadeless crown of every hue,
That never was seen when life's skies were blue?

MISCELLANEOUS.

DREAM-WORLD.

WHEN soft slumber hushes the soul in repose,
And the curtain unfolds where the dream-world
glows,
And the phantoms of fancy, with strange behests,
Move solemn and slow, like funeral guests, —
Then above and about there's a mystic gleam,
Like the flash of the stars on a rippling stream;
There's a moment of darkness, a silence intense,
And the glory of Eden entrances the sense.

Then we wander away
To the woodland hill,
And bathe in the spray
Of the mountain rill;
And rest in the shades
Of the odorous grove,
Where all is as pure
As the spirit of love, —
Where the sunlight sleeps
In a sparkling tide,
In the floral halls
Of the mountain-side, —
Where the west wind gathers
The breath of the flowers,
And wafts the perfume
Through the greenwood bowers, —
Beneath the green oak's leafy dome,
Through the sunny hours,
We make our home,

And trace the labyrinths, under the trees,
    With the Dryades.

    Ages seem rolling by,
    Dim to the sense ;
    Measureless treasures lie
    Through the immense
    Of delight ; to the sight,
    Brighter the vision grows,
    Clearer Elysian flows,
As, in soft slumbers, Time numbers the night.

    Then the soul is filled
    With a new desire,
    With the musical thrum
    Of Collina's lyre,
    And the pæans that come,
    In ravishing notes,
    From the plumy throats

Of the mountain choir;
And the varied voice
Of the balmy breeze,
Humming its murmur
Among the trees,
Wafts them away
Where the echoes stay,
Whispering melodies all the way.

Then away from the mountain,
Away from the hills,
To the foamy fountain
Of many rills,
Where the sunbeams glance
On the silvery sea,
And the nereids dance
To the melodie
Of the wind-harp's swelling,
That never is hushed

In its billowy dwelling;
Singing so sprightly,
Floating so lightly,
Over the waves of the silvery sea.

Then down through the tide,
To the coral grove,
Where the solemn-eyed fishes
In unrest rove,
To the twilighted halls
Of the coral caves,
Deep under the surge
Of the wayward waves,
To Doris' dominions,
Down under the waves.

There, in the coral glades
Under the sea,
In the soft twilight's shades
We shall be free,

With the bright water-sprite
Seeking new pleasures where
Thetis' treasures are,
Under the billows and pillows of light.

Then the columns of coral
  Will throw back the ray,
Through the sea-valleys floral,
  And halls of the fay.
Then upward we sweep,
From the waveless deep,
Where the storms are torpescent,
And the waters, quiescent,
  In solitude sleep.

On winged lightnings flying,
  We heavenward rise,
Ecstatic, erratic,
  Up-scaling the skies.

Here we see Purity
In beauty dwelling where,
(Happiness quelling care,)
Nothing can ever dissever the free.

Still onward and upward,
Through the azure of night,
To the realms of Urania, —
Her palace of light;
Baptizing the soul
In its magical flight,
In the tremulous comet's
Electrical light.

Thus purified, soar
To a region of glory,
Surpassing the more
Modest bloom of Aurora,
To a region so measureless,

Astrea with thee,
Leaving the treasureless
Earth and the sea,
For the bosom of love
Where the loved ones be.

Here we find those we knew
When life was gay,
Ere death had ventured to
Snatch them away.
Now will thy spirit sigh
In the re-union thrill,
With sweet communion, till
The dawn of the morn leads us down from the sky.

Suddenly changing, they
Fade from the sight:
Gone, like a cloud, away
Is our delight.

Lethe's stream drowns the dream,
  Yet Memory treasures all,
  Till we the pleasures call,
And from Elysian the vision redeem.

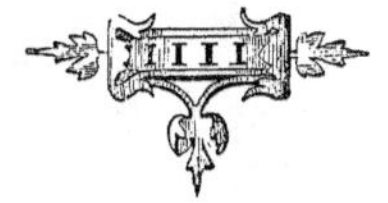

THE MOONLIGHT SERENADE.

'TWAS a bliss sublime,
In the olden time,
When the lover was suffered his love to tell,
To list to the chime
Of the music and rhyme
That came from the love-song's ritornel;
And nought was so sweet to the Spanish maid
As the song of the moonlight serenade.

How the maiden sighed
As her lover hied

To the open casement, or lattice bower!
It was sweet to her soul,
The erotic roll
Of fervor that flowed from his wild guitar;
But many a maiden has been betrayed
By the song of the moonlight serenade.

There's a legended tale,
How a father did wail
And weep for the loss of Zetella, his child.
She was beauteous and fair,
But too fond of night-air,
When its waving vibrations with music was wild;
For a gnome was the lover who sang and played
The song of the moonlight serenade.

And nightly there
Resounded the air
With the mystic melody love will inspire;

The gnome he played,
And Zetella prayed
For the kind consent of her aged sire;
But the sire, alas! was not to be swayed
By the song of the moonlight serenade.

One night, when the moon
Had vanished too soon,
Thus sang the weird gnome: "Zetella dear,
Oh! come with me
Far over the sea,
And we of thy sire shall have nothing to fear,
For I will be with thee: then be not afraid,
For love is the burthen of my serenade.

"There is untold worth
In the vaults of earth,
And beauties that fade not away with time;
And we'll banish woe
From our home below,

And thou shalt be queen over all the clime.
Then haste thee away." Zetella obeyed
The gnome, and his moonlight serenade.

Then her beauty did fade,
For her home was made
Deep down in the earth in the sunless cells,
Where love cheers not
The crystalline grot,
In a dark, dank region where love never dwells;
And she found, too late, she had been betrayed
By the song of the moonlight serenade.

Now, maidens, beware
How you breathe the night-air,
When there floats on its bosom your own bosom's sigh,
Or you'll feel the keen smart
Of a wound in your heart,
Which you've no way to heal but to lie down and die;
For many a maiden has been betrayed
By the song of the moonlight serenade.

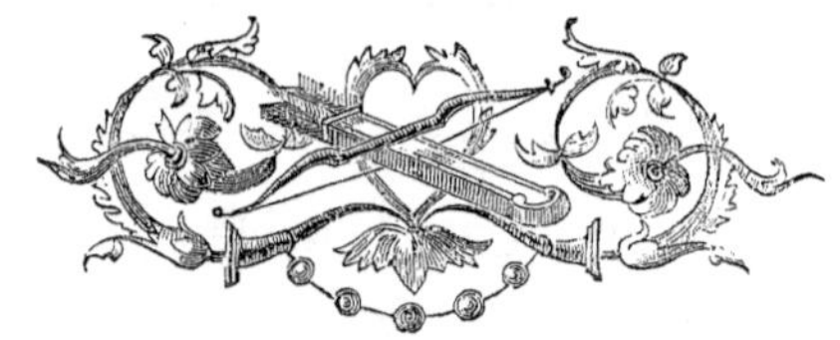

AUTUMN'S LESSON.

THE leaves are falling,
And summer flowers
Have ceased to blossom
In summer bowers,
And the zephyrs no more dally
With the lilies of the valley,
With the peonies and pansies,
With the buttercups and daisies,
In the groves and in the mazes
Of the meadow; but the weary wind is sighing,
Through all the trembling trees,

Day and night, and night and day,
With a fearful prophesying
Of the dying summer day;
And the ominous scarlet blaze
Of the fading forest trees
Is the robe of solemn Death,
As he rides upon the melancholy breeze,
And the misty, feathery haze
Is his breath,—
Is the winding-sheet of Summer, sunny Summer;
And the mellifluous notes
That were welling from the throats
Of the polyphonian choir,
That made the violet air
So palpitate with music,
Now are silent. Everywhere
Is swelling the knelling of the Summer's sunny hours.

I feel the solemn warning,
I hear the hollow moan

Of the never-weary wind,
With its mournful monotone;
And I listen to the humming,
As the chordless anthem rolls;
And I listen to the thrumming
Of the lyre of the ghouls,
As it tells of decay,—
As it tallies on our souls
Every moment passed away.
Oh! is there not a flower that can stay?
Not a leaf, not a spray,
That shall weave a summer way,
Full of beauty, full of bloom,
Through the weary winter's gloom?
Oh! must the north wind's breath
Scatter death,
Scatter doom,
Scatter all our hope of life,
In the strife,

As it hurries, thus, the living to the tomb?—
Hurries, thus, the Summer and her flowers,
To the shadow of the never-counted hours?

Then a spirit, that is keeping
Solemn vigils in my bosom, with its weeping,
Seems to say,
"Thou art hasting, thus, away,
In thy dreaming, to the tomb;
Passing, like the fading flowers,
That ne'er again shall bloom
In summer bowers.
Thus, too, there may
Be sorrow, grief, and sighing
When thou shalt pass away;
When the ties of earth are broken,
And the loved ones of thy bosom shall appear,
And offer the last token
Of their love, and gather round thy bier,

Moaning, weeping, sighing,
When thou shalt pass away, — art dying, —
Never to see again the day for ever!

But the storms of winter go,
And the sun will melt the snow;
There is music in the air,
There is beauty in the bowers, —
Song and beauty everywhere
Woven in the sunny hours;
And the May-time comes again,
With all her smiling train
Of animated life,
Banishing the sighing, banishing the strife,
Waking all the legions of the embryotic flowers, —
Waking into living all the flowers and the trees,
And the voices of the breeze
Are merging into murmurs of delight;
They are whispering their plight,

Through all the glowing hours, —
Through the silence of the night, —
To the budding and the bursting of the flowers,
From earth and skies
Thanksgivings rise,
For that blest law that God doth give,
That all may die to live.

Shall not I as well as they?
Then a spirit that is dwelling
In my bosom, with its swelling,
Seems to say,
"From the darkness of the tomb
(Inevitable doom),
All life shall bloom again,
Free from sorrow, free from pain,
Free from the north wind's breath,
Free from the blight of death,
In a sweet May-land above

All the threatening of the night,
And the yearning after light,
Above life's chilling snow,
Above the bosom's woe,
Where thy spirit shall,
  Shall inherit
All the fragrance of that flower that the angels christen
  love."

IDYLIA.

I'VE built my love a bower on the lawn,
And I have sprinkled roses on the roof,
And thyme upon the floor, and since the dawn,
Have wove the honeysuckle in the woof.

And now arises on the waving air
The sweet perfume of morning's dewy breath,
While I am watching, from love's rosy lair,
To see Idylia tripping o'er the heath.

She promised she would meet me at the bower;
She promised, too, that it should not be late;
Yet I've been mourning through this weary hour,
As mourns the turtle for his tardy mate.

A light step trips along the dewy hill,
A sweet voice echoes o'er the sunny lea :
I know it by its ever-merry trill ;
I know the echoes by their tones of glee.

And she has hastened till her face is flushed
With softest tints of morning's rosy glow ;
The lark is still, the linnet's voice is hushed,
To hear awhile such rapturous music flow.

Besprinkled o'er her brow of pearly white,
The pouting drops of crystal lie at rest,
And sparkle in the rainbow-tinted light,
Like diamond dew upon the lily's crest.

"Ah! I have waited here for thee so long,
And I have listened for thine airy tread,
And I had thought to chide thee when that song
Of gladness from thy rosy lip had fled.

"Come rest thee now within this fragrant bower;
Come wreathe thy tiny fingers, love, in mine,
As I have wreathed the roses for this hour,
While deeming every robin's note was thine.

"Come, twine thy tresses round my bosom, love,
And lay thy head where it so often lies,
That I may watch the tangled hues above
Reflected in the depths of thy blue eyes."

CAMBAHEE.

DOWN upon the dancing river,
Cambahee,
Dwelt together I and Eva
Happily;
Other bliss we never sought,
Of no other pleasures thought,
Than to know two loving souls,
Full of glee,
Dwelt together on the shoals
Of Cambahee.

But a sad and solemn order
                    Came to me
From the chieftain of the border
                    Of the sea.
In the land where Eva dwelt,
Tyrant Saxon swords were felt:
Kisses, then, and tears, from Eva
                    Flowed as free
As the ripples of the river
                    Cambahee.

By my side the youthful braves
                    Fought and fell,
Till the blood, like water-waves,
                    Drenched the dell.
Onward rushed the foemen strong,
Treading to the battle-song,
Till I feared that my sweet Eva,
                    Far from me,

Would be driven forth for ever
From Cambahee.

'Mid the carnage, dust, and smoke,
There was one,
Strange and wild, whose ready stroke
Praises won;
And when foemen round me pressed,
Blows were broken by the breast
Of that strange one: it was Eva!
Woe is me!
Love is lost, and joy for ever,
On Cambahee!

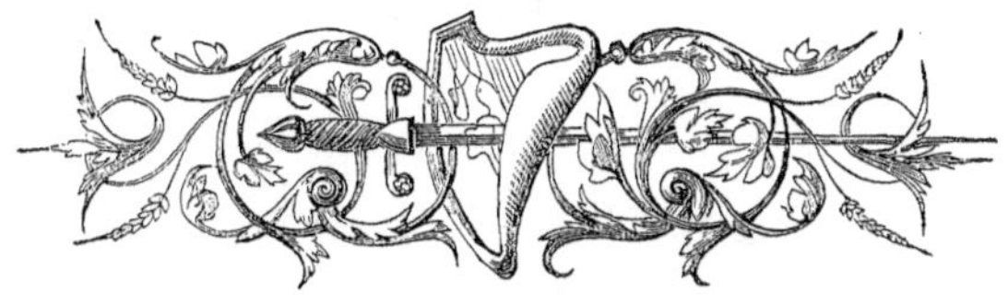

THE TEAR-SPIRIT.

I CAME when the night-bird was singing
  Her song in the dell,
And Echo was busily flinging
The notes where the tomb-spirits dwell,
In their sepulchre-cell,
When the old church-bell was ringing
So solemn, and mournfully bringing
On my spirit a mystical spell.
'Twas the church where Minora was wedded,
Where the warp of his love was threaded
With the woof of his bride's, and well;
The bell that chimed his knell,

That tolled when Minora was bedded
In the earth, where every one dreaded
To look in his sepulchre-cell,
To bid him a final farewell.

Then I sat down in sorrow beside it, —
In grief, beside his cold grave.
My sorrow, I wished not to hide it;
My anguish, I scarce could abide it;
And the tear-drops my wan cheek did lave:
The grief-token, how could I chide it?
So his heart, it drank up the tear-wave
That trickled down on his cold grave.

Then arose to my vision a vapor,
A mist that came up from his tomb:
And it came like the flame of the taper,
The foxfire lights in the gloom;
And it said, "Thy love is requited,
The tomb his love has not blighted,

The grave your loves cannot part!"
Then I knew, by my own bosom's swelling,
The tomb is not made for love's dwelling,
The grave's not a home for the heart,
And our souls shall again be united
Where the loving and loved never part.

FOUR DEGREES OF LOVE.

I ASKED a prattling infant, while it played
Upon its mother's bosom with delight,
And while the golden tresses careless strayed
Around its chubby shoulders, pure and white:
"What feel'st thou for thy mother, gentle dove?"
It smiled in innocence, and lisped, "'Tis love."

I asked a beauteous girl, as bright and pure
As fresh-blown roses of a summer day, —
Nor grief nor sadness from her eye could lure
A tear her smiling did not chase away,

For with despair her youthful heart ne'er strove, —
"What makes thee glad?" She, laughing, answered,
"Love."

I asked a maid, whose eye had ceased to glow,
Or light the beauty of her faded cheek,
While Melancholy sat upon her brow,
And grief was in her smile, — the pathway bleak
Wherein with maiden fortitude she strove, —
"What mars thy peace?" She faintly whispered, "Love."

I asked a faithful wife, — whose constant care
To cheer the loved one was her greatest pleasure;
Who strove incessantly that she might share
That love that was her dearest earthly treasure,
For Virtue round their hearts her chaplet wove, —
"What sweetens woman's toil?" She answered, "Love."

THE POET-ZONE.

TOILING in the night-time,
Toiling by the light
Of the taper, on the paper,
Through the weary night;
All along the land-marks,
Through the great unknown,
There the eager poet wanders
With his soul alone,
Reaching, writing, heart inditing,
Weary waiting for the lighting
Of the poet-zone.

Down among the karl-kings
Of the humid earth,
Where the fountain of the mountain
Had its primal birth;
Up among the star-lights,
Glinting in the blue,
Roving through the rainbows
Of supernal dew,
Seeking treasure for his measure, —
Seeking evanescent pleasure, —
In the poet-zone.

Raving, in his unrest,
With delicious pain,
Embryotic thought, erotic,
Rushes through his brain;
And the taunting soul-guide,
Wayward ciceron',
Toles the tireless spirit where

Pierian pearls are strown,
To the ages of the sages,
Of the antiquated pages
Of the poet-zone.

Striving for the soul-thought
Burning in his brow,
Barely breathing, rarely wreathing,
Rhyme and rhythm flow;
And with hurried heart-beats,
Rolling one by one,
Weaves the mystic monologues
In a monotone;
Culling any of the many
Beauties of the miscellany
Of the poet-zone.

GLOOM AND BLOOM.

THE day is dark, and cloud and gloom
Throw solemn shadows in my room;
The music of the gentle rain
Has ceased its patter on the pane,
And shriller shrieks and wilder song
Are swept by Borean winds along:
But still the sun is shining high
Above the melancholy sky.

The angry clouds are floating low;
The woods are swaying to and fro;

A deeper gloom, a deeper shade,
Is on the meadow, hill, and glade;
I feel, though dark the shadows fall,
My heart is sadder than them all:
But still the sun is shining high
Above the melancholy sky.

DAISY.

MY Daisy is a darling girl,
With heart so true,
And o'er her neck hangs many a curl
Of golden hue;
And then her eyes, — such beamy eyes, —
As liquid as the azure skies,
And a stormy sparkle in them lies,
That thrills me through;
But I'll not tell you of the trance
She throws me into with their glance.
Why should I, if I could? — and, true,
How could I, if I wanted to?

My Daisy's like the little bird
                    That skims the air:
Sure such a voice was never heard, —
                    So rich and rare:
'Tis sweeter than a tunèd lute,
More liquid than the mellow flute;
And when she sings, the lark is mute,
                    The linnets stare;
But I'll not tell how full and free
It warbled when she plighted me.
Why should I, if I could? — and, true,
How could I, if I wanted to?

My Daisy, she is blithe and fair,
                    And fresh and free,
And then she has a jaunty air
                    That pleases me;
Her cheek is like the dewy rose,
Her teeth as white as mountain snows;

Her limbs are lithe, and no one knows
So well as she —
But I'll not tell you of the bliss
That floods me with her modest kiss.
Why should I, if I could? — and, true,
How could I, if I wanted to?

My Daisy's good, my Daisy's true
As true can be;
Her love is fresh as morning dew,
And she loves me.
Modest as a May-night moon,
Brilliant as the sun at noon,
I shall marry Daisy soon,
And then you'll see —
But I'll not give you further sign,
For Daisy's but a dream of mine.
Why should I, if I could? — and, true,
How could I, if I wanted to?

NARCISSUS AND PHOTOGRAPHY.

NARCISSUS, one day,
As mythologies say,
Was hunting a buck on the bank of a river,
When, tired of the chase,
He slackened his pace,
And threw on the turf his bow and his quiver,
And sat down beside them on the mossy brink,
And leaned himself over to lave and to drink.

The water was clear,
And, as he drew near,
Exquisitely imaged each delicate feature.

He was somewhat amazed
At the bright eyes that gazed
From the archèd brow of a beautiful creature;
And his wonder increased when he saw those eyes
Answer his glance with the same surprise.

The first impulse was this, —
To snatch a sweet kiss;
Quite natural, too, as the liquid he tipples;
But his rosy-hued lips
Had scarce touched their tips,
When the waves away darted in concentric ripples,
And a hundred distorted faces, or more,
Hurried away to the opposite shore.

Then, day after day,
He wandered away
To gaze at himself in the beautiful river:
'Twas his Eden now,
And the buck and the roe

Needed no flight from his bow and his quiver;
So the silly youth strove to get rid of himself,
Just to hug to his bosom his shadowy elf.

Then he pined away,
For the love, they say,
Of his own sweet self, who didn't return it;
And he wept by the side
Of the crystal tide,
In the hope that perhaps his devotion might earn it;
Till at last, as he watched by his shadowy bride,
Worn out with the love of himself, he died.

Then Jupiter, true
To his subject's due,
Changed the youth to a beautiful flower;
And Apollo declared,
If he should be spared
An age or two longer, he'd have the power
To paint the image of all who may
Call upon him in the proper way.

MYRENE.

I HAVE a picture of Myrene:
Fairer one was never seen.
Note the waves of golden hair
Creeping o'er her bosom fair;
Mark the lustre of her eyes,
Glowing like the starry skies, —
Eyes that seem communing now,
Speaking from her thoughtful brow, —
Speaking bliss no one may tell, —
Bliss, alas! I knew too well.
Though the Fates decree we part,
I wear this image next my heart.

She was fair to look upon
As an houri; and I won,
As the sunlight wins the dew,
All the love her bosom knew.
Days of joy went noiseless by,
As the twilight leaves the sky.
When the faintest ray was gone,
Came the night without a dawn,
Shutting from my soul the sheen
Of the blue eyes of Myrene;
Yet, though for another sphere
She has left me drooping here,
Two joys are mine, and they are sighs,
And gazing on her pictured eyes.

SUMMER MORNING.

I.

ALL hushed and still, the voiceless air
Is sleeping in the vale;
The morning rises fresh and fair,
Like a veilèd nun from holy prayer,
And her dewy light is pale.

II.

Aurora now, in robes of red,
And chariot of fire,
Arises from her azure bed,
With torch of flame by Phœbus fed,
And lights the gloomy pyre.

III.

And, soaring up the starry dome,
  Out-blooms each starry ray,
Proclaiming from her mystic tome,
The glorious god of day has come,
  To chase the gloom away.

IV.

The blushes on her brow of light,
  The crimson of her crest,
That lights the interlunar night,
Are melting to a pearly white,
  Adown the distant west.

V.

The summer sun, in mellow hues,
  The landscape now is steeping;
The fleet Aurora still pursues;
While kissing up the crystal dews,
  The night-flowers have been weeping.

VI.

The merry lark, with song of praise,
  Has scaled the misty wall,
And laves her in the genial rays,
And sings her merry matin lays,
  Above the floating pall.

VII.

All nature, smiling, ushers in,
  From midnight's silent sadness,
The purple morn with sandals green,
The summer morn, so fair and sheen,
  With notes of joy and gladness.

SONGS.

MUSIC OF THE DRUM.

I.

COME, soldiers, come to the rolling of the drum,—
To the clatter and the batter of the spirit-stirring drum.
How the furious music rolls!
How it thrills our very souls!
For there's battle in the rattle of the drum, drum, drum.

II.

At the rolling of the drum will every soldier come,
With his palpitating bosom keeping measure to the drum;

And every step he takes,
And every move he makes,
Is responding to the pounding of the drum, drum, drum.

III.

When he bursts into the battle, and the fiery foemen come,
Then his feet are wafted onward by the swelling of the drum.
For the soldier's soul is rife
With the warble of the fife,
And the rolling and the trolling of the drum, drum, drum.

IV.

For when he hears the hum of the rapid-rolling drum, —
The reverberating rattle of the clamorous kettle-drum, —
He can brave the cannon's roar,
He can rush through fields of gore,
To the humming and the drumming of the drum, drum, drum.

V.

And when the battle's ended, and the cannon's mouth is dumb,

Then his weary limbs will rally at the rattle of the drum;
For the wounded must be dressed,
And the lost be laid to rest
With a muffle on the ruffle of the drum, drum, drum.

VI.

Then the weary mourners come to the murmur of the drum,—
To the sad and solemn measure of the melancholy drum;
When the music sinks and swells,
What a world of woe it tells,
In the surges of the dirges of the drum, drum, drum!

VII.

Then come, soldiers, come to the rolling of the drum,
To the clatter and the batter of the spirit-stirring drum.
How the furious music rolls!
How it thrills our very souls!
For there's battle in the rattle of the drum, drum, drum.

THE OLD SCHOOL-HOUSE.

I.

WHERE the land slopes down to a little brook,
That prattles its way from a sylvan nook
In the mountain side; where the summer breeze
Toys with the leaves of the maple-trees,
And the robin and wren, with song ever new,
Warble their music the whole day through, —
Just over the bridge by the old saw-mill
Stands a little red school-house under the hill.

II.

Ah! well I remember those school-day times,
When life was a flow of brook-like rhymes.
The house was small, and the benches spare,
But those who filled them were fresh and fair;
And many a lesson my bosom took,
That was not learned from the spelling-book:
These dreams of the past are with me still,
That were dreamed in the school-house under the hill.

III.

Long years since then have passed away,
And the old school-house has gone to decay;
The sagging boards of paint are shorn,
And the slanting gables are weather-worn;
And there are holes, in the roof about,
Where the owl and bat go in and out,
And that is so sad to think of: still,
'Tis the same old school-house under the hill.

IV.

As I gaze at the house, all shattered and gray,
It beckons me up the little foot-way,
That once was so pleasant, now a mass
Of darnels and thistles and tangled grass;
So I pass, with a shudder, the creaking door,
And daintily, orderly, cross the floor,
And glide to the seat I once did fill
In the little red school-house under the hill.

V.

Then scenes long past arise to my view,
And the days of my boyhood come back anew;
And I hear the buzz of the busy school,
And the sharp rat-tat of the master's rule;
The classes come on to the floor again,
With the stalwart boy at the foot, as then;
And again the jubilant voices fill
The little red school-house under the hill.

VI.

Then I play the tricks that I used to play
When the master's face was turned away;
And again, as I stand at the head of the class,
I miss the word that *she* may pass,
And I catch the glow of her modest eyes;
It is ample pay for the quarter's prize;
She wins with a blush, I lose with a thrill
Of pride, in the school-house under the hill.

VII.

The vision is over: the *present* is here;
I leave the old seat with a parting tear,
For never again will the flush and prime
Of youth come back to that golden time;
The little bird's song is a plaintive moan,
And the trill of the brook has a solemn tone;
Yet memories prompt me to linger still
By the little red school-house under the hill.

VIII.

Like thee, old house, I am shattered and gray,
And I wonder, when I shall pass away,
If ever a heart will cherish, for me,
Memories as dear as mine for thee.
I turn away, with a last fond look
At the green hill-slopes and the murmuring brook,
And the crumbling doors and the rotting sill
Of the little red school-house under the hill.

THE SPIRIT-BRIDE.

I.

I WANDERED forth, one starry night,
Along the woodland hill,
Where Cynthia's pure and placid light
Was glancing on the rill.
I trod alone, in pensive mood,
The beamy water's side,
And saw, in that sweet solitude,
My soul's ideal bride.

II.

About her form, a halo bright
Of lucid radiance fell;

As rays of noonday's streaming light
  Dart in a darkened cell.
I knew it was a dream, and yet
  I nestled by her side;
So happy I, that I had met
  My own, my spirit-bride.

III.

We wandered through a summer way,
  Where bliss and beauty reign,
And revelled in that endless day
  Beyond the land of pain.
" That blessed love and glorious light,
  That death cannot divide,
Is all for us beyond life's night,"
  Thus said my spirit-bride.

IV.

We wandered through a summer clime,
  Where loved ones never sigh;

And as we loved in childhood's time,
  So loved we in the sky.
Nor till Aurora's rosy glance
  The azure dome had dyed,
Did Reason wake me from the trance
  And steal my spirit-bride.

V.

Was it a fantasy, — a dream, —
  That in my brain had birth,
And has no type, and yet doth seem
  As real as the earth?
I know it was a dream, and yet
  To truth is so allied,
That I should feel a keen regret
  To lose my spirit-bride.

LOVE'S SYMBOLS.

I.

WHEN the light breezes blow,
So gentle and low,
Weaving sweet melodies into the hours,
They breathe the perfume
Of the lilies that bloom
In the sunlighted valleys and dew-dripping bowers;
And they whisper to me of a heart ever true,
As the lily whose petals unfold to the dew;
And that heart is all mine, with its love and perfume,
Till the winds cease to blow, and the lilies to bloom.

II.

When the stars, rising bright
In the azure of night,
Smile sweet on my soul from their blue homes above,
I read, in their sheen,
Of a beautiful queen,
Whose heart is a kingdom of ravishing love;
And that kingdom and queen, and that heart ever true
As the glow of the stars in the fathomless blue,
In the bloom of their beauty for ever are mine,
Till the sky fades away, and the stars cease to shine.

III.

When the sun, riding high
In the luminous sky,
Is pledging the earth with his amorous fire,
And the flowers and the trees,
As they bend to the breeze,
Drink life, light, and beauty with ardent desire,

They tell of a heart that is true to its own,
As the earth to the sun since the sun ever shone;
And that heart, with its life, light, and beauty, is mine,
Till the earth lose her bloom, and the sun fails to shine.

EMBLEMS OF LIBERTY.

I.

ALL hail to the nation whose freemen and foemen
Are bound by the deeds that our fathers have done!
Where the voice of the lord is the voice of the yeomen,
Whose million of bosoms are beating as one!
And blest be those heroes whom fondly we cherish,
Whose blood set the seal on the hearts of the free!
And this seal of our liberty never can perish
While the monarch that rules is the *vox populi.*

II.

Wave, flag of our freedom! thy bright stars shall glimmer,
A type of the time of our liberty's might;

And the sheen of their glory shall never grow dimmer
  While their prototypes smile in the azure of night.
And the stripes? Ah! each ominous stripe is a token
  Of terror to all who may dare to invade;
For this union of bosoms can never be broken,
  These emblems of liberty never will fade.

III.

And beauty is bright in this land of our glory,
  Where honored and blest are the idols of love,
As placid and pure as the blush of Aurora,
  And chaste as the cherubs that hover above.
Oh! each sentry-arm is a guard to its treasure;
  Each heart is a home that is true to its own.
Love, union, and liberty! Time cannot measure
  This trine of our nation of many in one.

IV.

And here are the hills that from ocean to ocean
  Reach up to the sky, and partake of its sheen;

While the rivers and brooks hum the country's devotion,
  Through the grain-gleaming valleys that slumber between ;
And these mountains and valleys and rivers we cherish,
  As emblems of union that never shall wane ;
And as soon will these types of our liberty perish,
  As this land of our glory be severed in twain.

THE TEMPLE OF BEAUTY.

I.

I HAVE found out the Temple of Beauty;
  I have seen where fair Innocence dwells,—
Where Virtue holds sentinel duty
  O'er the passions that Love never quells;
And nought can compare with that palace,
  Where modest-eyed Innocence dwells.

II.

I found out this truth by a token,—
  A token that beamed from thine eye,

When the throb of thy bosom had woken
  The love that came forth on a sigh ;
And no language was ever yet spoken
  That with that soft language can vie.

III.

Idylia's that Temple of Beauty ;
  Its vestal, her virtue divine ;
And I'll sacrifice love, as a duty,
  At the shrine of this loved one of mine ;
It is more than the pleasure of duty
  To bow to so holy a shrine.

IV.

She is fair as the flowers that blossom
  In the reign of the rosy May-queen ;
That bloom on the beautiful bosom
  Of the May, in her mantle of green ;
That embroider, with harmonied garlands,
  Her vesture of velveted green.

V.

Like the language these flowers have spoken
  Is the voice of her being to me,
And remembrance remains as a token
  Of bliss that for ever shall be ;
And the love-tie shall never be broken
  That binds my beloved to me.

LINDEN BOWERS.

I.

THERE is a gently flowing stream
Among the linden bowers:
Its depths are full of floating green,
Its banks are fringed with flowers;
And by this stream there is a way, —
A pleasant path along, —
And every day comes Emma May
To cheer it with her song.
I love this little maiden too,
As she trips through the grove;
But then I could not tell her so,
Though it should win her love.

II.

Her heart is true, her eyes are blue
  As is the azure sky;
Her lips are like the rose's hue;
  And then I heard her sigh,
And sing a gentle love-refrain,
  The airy little elf,
I know she loves me back again,
  And keeps it to herself.
I gaze on her with fond delight,
  She looks so shy at me:
Oh! isn't this the saddest plight
  In which two hearts could be?

III.

The humbird does not fear to tell
  How much he loves the flowers;
The soft winds kiss the lily-bell,
  Through all the summer hours;

And then how well the cooing dove
  Can win his loving mate!
While we must shun each other's love
  Till it will be too late.
But she and I will sigh and sigh,
  And make this world so bleak,
I wish that either she or I
  Was bold enough to speak.

THE PICTURE THAT HANGS ON THE WALL.

I.

OUR Lily was fair as a fairy,
As modest and meek as a dove,
As placid and pure as a peri,
But her heart it was fuller of love.
Ah! merry was she as a swallow,
And her smile it was sweeter than all
The smiles that the painter Apollo
Ever pencilled to hang on the wall.

II.

Then we trimmed up her bonny brown tresses,
  While her dimples sunk down in a smile;
Dressed her up in the best of her dresses,
  And laughed at her glee all the while.
And we called her our sweet little swallow,
  The bonniest beauty of all,
And we smiled as the painter Apollo
  Traced her picture to hang on the wall.

III.

But Lily grew pale, just to teach us
  That heaven had a claim on its own;
And we feared that the duplicate features
  Of Lily would soon be alone.
Then her eye it grew fainter and fainter;
  And her voice lost the trill in its call;
So we blessed, then, Apollo the painter,
  For the picture that hangs on the wall.

IV.

Now Lily lies under the roses,
  That wearily wave at her head;
But she heeds not that where she reposes
  Is chilly, for Lily is dead:
And this picture, that never may perish,
  Is all that is left of her, — all;
And, oh, how the image we cherish
  Of Lily, that hangs on the wall!

THE JUNE AND THE MOON.

I.

'TWAS a summer-night moon,
And the month was June,
The daisies were hiding their heads in the grass,
When I plighted my love,
In the moon-lighted grove,
To Mary, the rosy-cheeked lass.
As the day she was bright,
And as fair as the night
Over-sprinkled with stars; but the charm
Of the hour to me
Was the bonny blue e'e
Of the maiden that hung on my arm.

II.

I spoke of the boon
That some moon-lighted June
Should grant me, and prayed that the time might be nigh.
She smiled, and said,
As she turned her head
And roguishly gazed in my eye, —
" The June is here,
And the moon shines clear" —
I kissed off the sentence with glee.
Since then many Junes,
And many fair moons,
Have smiled on my Mary and me.

TEMPUS FUGIT.

I.

TEMPUS FUGIT! Let it fly:
What's the use of whining?
Better far to laugh than cry,
Or always be repining.
Why regret the passing year?
The world is what we make it,
And Time will always bring us cheer,
If we've the heart to take it.

II.

Tempus fugit! More's the need
That we watch the treasure;
Every moment brings its meed
Of profit and of pleasure.
Let us bear with toil and care?
The world is full of beauty, —
Peace and plenty everywhere, —
If we do our duty.

III.

Tempus fugit! Day by day,
Never once receding,
Let us follow in the way,
This great lesson heeding, —
Never weary: time goes on,
In sunshine and in shadow;
Onward you, till you have won
The wished-for El Dorado.

IV.

Tempus fugit! No delay
  For your sighs and sinnings;
If you linger by the way,
  You will miss the innings.
Then be noble, just, and true:
  You will never rue it;
The world will be the better, too,
  That you have once passed through it.

www.ingramcontent.com/pod-product-compliance
Lightning Source LLC
LaVergne TN
LVHW011218110826
845150LV00006B/1465

* 9 7 8 1 4 2 5 5 1 6 7 2 7 *